Saint Francis of Assisi Speaks

Published by Abba Books LLC
abbabooksllc@gmail.com
Copyright © 2023 Marie-Josée Thibault

All Rights Reserved

No part of this publication may be reproduced, distributed, or transmitted in any form or by any means, including photocopying, recording, or other electronic or mechanical methods, without the prior written permission of the publisher.

First Edition, 2023
Designed and Edited by Abba Books LLC
ISBN: 979-8-9897259-5-3

Abba Books LLC
34972 Newark Blvd, #441
Newark, CA 94560

www.abbamyfatheriloveyou.com
https://www.facebook.com/AbbaILoveYouBooks/

Thy Peace on Earth must be achieved. No light, no litany must be spared to honor Thy Grace.
-Saint Paul

Table of Contents

Preface____VI	Chap12____27	Chap24____55	Chap36____87
Chap1____1	Chap13____29	Chap25____57	Chap37____89
Chap2____3	Chap14____31	Chap26____61	Chap38____91
Chap3____5	Chap15____33	Chap27____63	Chap39____93
Chap4____7	Chap16____37	Chap28____65	Chap40____95
Chap5____9	Chap17____39	Chap29____67	Chap41____99
Chap6____13	Chap18____41	Chap30____69	Chap42____101
Chap7____15	Chap19____43	Chap31____73	Chap43____103
Chap8____17	Chap20____45	Chap32____77	Chap44____105
Chap9____19	Chap21____49	Chap33____79	Chap45____107
Chap10____21	Chap22____51	Chap34____81	Chap46____111
Chap11____25	Chap23____53	Chap35____83	

Preface

Readers of this collection from Heaven, welcome to this wonderfully edifying series written by Saint Francis of Assisi! I implore you to read these books on a daily basis as part of your devotional practice. This guide to Christian living is rich, unique, and perfectly adapted to modern life, spurred by the fact that Francis visits us regularly. He is aware of the exact sorrows and controversies that affect contemporary society. His instructions and training will be miraculously useful to you in your everyday life.

Francis is very gentle and humble when he visits me. His prayers are beautiful and transformative, and they arouse pain in the center of my left hand (unlike Padre Pio, whose visits arouse pain in the center of my right hand).

Live out all the lessons given in these blessed books and benefit from the consecration and extraordinary assistance of Saint Francis of Assisi!

Francis, I love you!

Marie-Josée

Saint Francis of Assisi Speaks

My children, my brothers and sisters, my friends in the Good News, I love you; listen to me well. Dear heart, do realize today, in the very depth of your heart, that the Father knows you personally much more than you do. He knows your strengths and flaws, your hopes and despairs, and most importantly, the deep motivation at the root of every emotion, every thought, every word, every gesture, and every work. He knows all about you, each and every one of you, because He created you! He created mankind and He knows only too well this thing that is the human. That is why He is able to forgive you, to correct you, and to teach you through His Messengers — and His Son is His Fundamental Messenger and the most Elevated One. Stay calm in any situation, especially those you regret bitterly due to negligence or error, and ask Mercy of God directly, with a contrite heart, to forgive this offense made against God and human beings, for an offense made against human beings is one and the same as an offense made against Him. Amen. Alleluia!

Saint Francis of Assisi Speaks

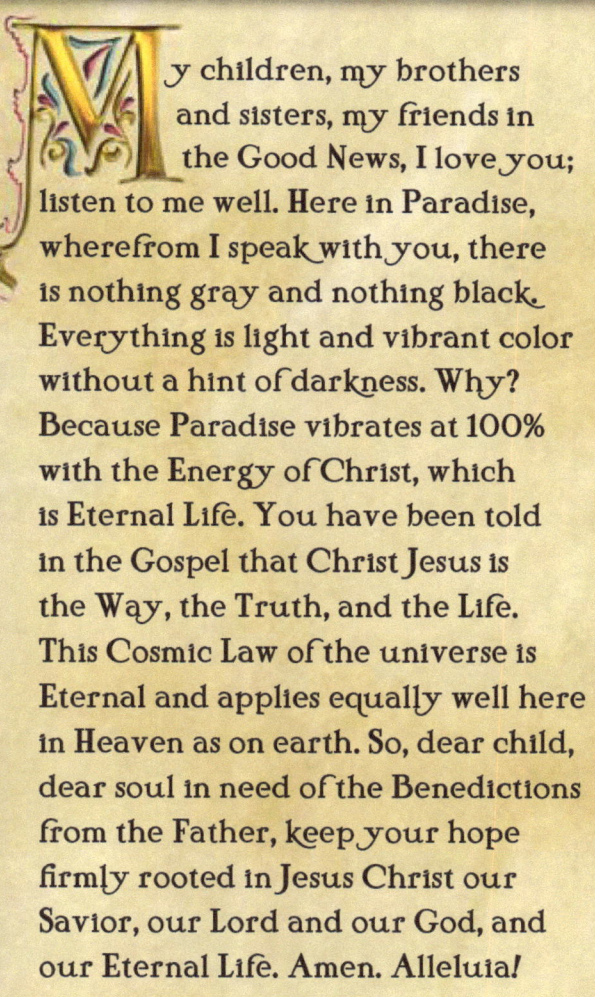

My children, my brothers and sisters, my friends in the Good News, I love you; listen to me well. Here in Paradise, wherefrom I speak with you, there is nothing gray and nothing black. Everything is light and vibrant color without a hint of darkness. Why? Because Paradise vibrates at 100% with the Energy of Christ, which is Eternal Life. You have been told in the Gospel that Christ Jesus is the Way, the Truth, and the Life. This Cosmic Law of the universe is Eternal and applies equally well here in Heaven as on earth. So, dear child, dear soul in need of the Benedictions from the Father, keep your hope firmly rooted in Jesus Christ our Savior, our Lord and our God, and our Eternal Life. Amen. Alleluia!

Saint Francis of Assisi Speaks

My children, my brothers and sisters, my friends in the Good News, I love you; listen to me well. Today, through the Holy Spirit, you will see me. Yes, dear friend, dear heart, the Father has authorized me to reveal myself to you as I please. Rejoice and be hopeful, be on the lookout, and keep your heart wide open for a visitation from myself in a very tangible and unique way for you. Pray, my children, pray, and you will be rewarded! Amen. Alleluia!

Saint Francis of Assisi Speaks

My children, my brothers and sisters, my friends in the Good News, I love you; listen to me well. Today, and for the rest of your life, remain under the Ray of Light given to you by the Holy Spirit. The Holy Spirit, dear friend, dear heart, is known here by the Name of God the Holy Spirit. He directs all the operations involving our Mystical relations with you, that is to say, all the relationships being established between the whole Heaven and earth, and this at all levels. Miracles received, unexpected solutions to your problems, profound and lasting conversions of hearts: all these beautiful phenomena and many others belong to the domain of God the Holy Spirit, the Comforting Spirit, the Anointing of God's Grace. Pray my friends, my dear children, pray to God the Holy Spirit with all your strength, and from the very depth of your heart, and the Mysteries of your life as well as the Mysteries of the Father and the Son will be revealed unto you! Amen. Alleluia!

Saint Francis of Assisi Speaks

My children, my brothers and sisters, my friends in the Good News, I love you; listen to me well. Today, my dear heart, forget and ignore completely what is happening outside of your physical body. Wrap yourself comfortably in your heart where your Heavenly Family awaits you, and stay with us all day! Here, my beautiful soul, is Paradise, and it is so good to live with the Almighty Father in His Kingdom! Stay with us in Paradise today! Amen. Alleluia!

Today, through the Holy Spirit, you will see me
~ Saint Francis

Saint Francis of Assisi Speaks

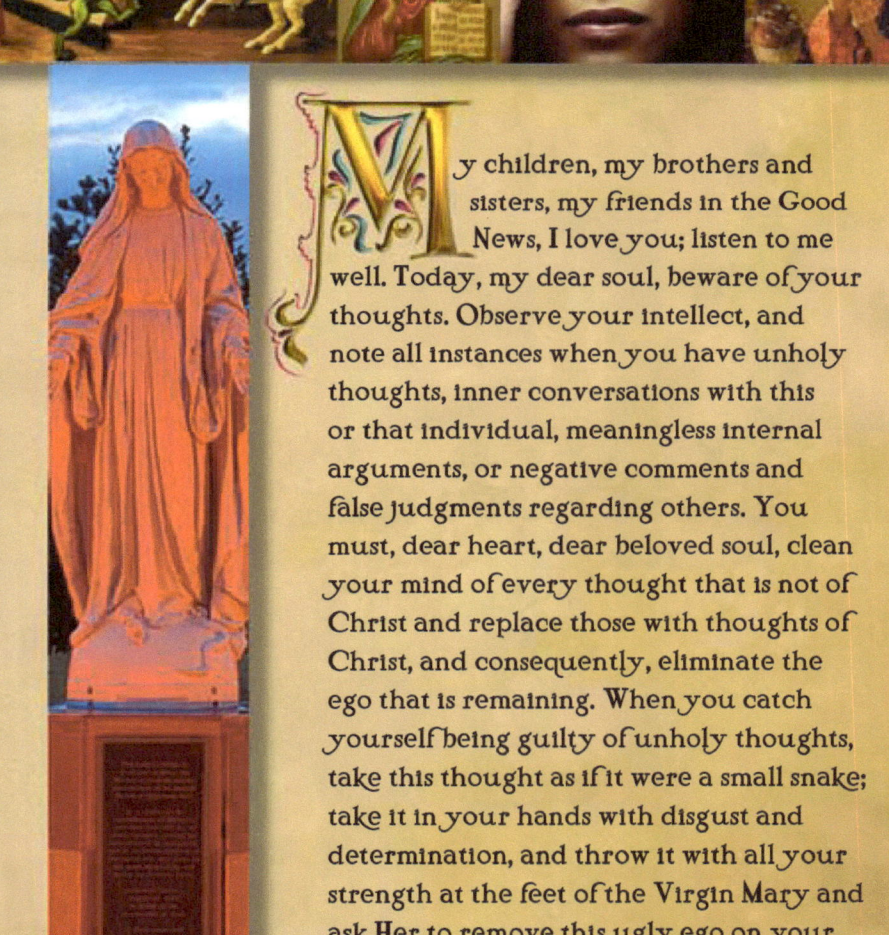

My children, my brothers and sisters, my friends in the Good News, I love you; listen to me well. Today, my dear soul, beware of your thoughts. Observe your intellect, and note all instances when you have unholy thoughts, inner conversations with this or that individual, meaningless internal arguments, or negative comments and false judgments regarding others. You must, dear heart, dear beloved soul, clean your mind of every thought that is not of Christ and replace those with thoughts of Christ, and consequently, eliminate the ego that is remaining. When you catch yourself being guilty of unholy thoughts, take this thought as if it were a small snake; take it in your hands with disgust and determination, and throw it with all your strength at the feet of the Virgin Mary and ask Her to remove this ugly ego on your behalf. Pray the Ave Maria three times. Repeat! Repeat! Repeat! And shortly, your intellect and your heart will be liberated! Amen. Alleluia!

Saint Francis of Assisi Speaks

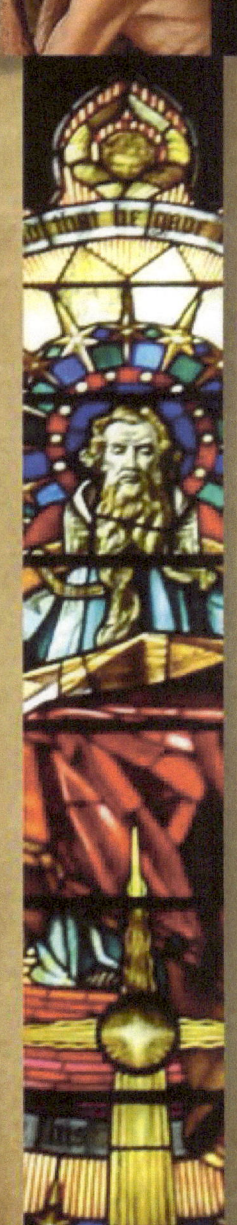

My children, my brothers and sisters, my friends in the Good News, I love you; listen to me well. Today, dear heart in distress because of life on earth, I want you to surrender to me — as well as to Christ Jesus and to God the Father Almighty — all your worries, your concerns, your questions, your pain, your disappointments, your shattered dreams: I take them all in my Divine Heart united to the One of Christ and of the Virgin Mary, and within the Holy Trinity. God's Plan is Powerful, God's Plan removes all obstacles, God's Plan performs Miracles every day. You are part of God's Plan. I say unto you, I say unto you verily, give me all your worries today, and in their place insert God's Plan, which will be revealed very quickly before your eyes. Amen. Alleluia!

Saint Francis of Assisi Speaks

My children, my brothers and sisters, my friends in the Good News, I love you; listen to me well. Today, dear heart, dear soul seeking God, give this day to God. God, Who has blessed you when you rose today and every day of your life, God Who created your soul at the very beginning of the Creation with Love and Respect for your unique personality, God Who prepares your return Home, his Kingdom in Heaven. Often say this prayer today and every day of your life: "Holy God, Blessed God, Immortal God, Strong God, Almighty God, God our Father, have Mercy on us and on the whole world." Repeat often during the day this simple prayer which greatly pleases God: "God the Father Almighty, I love you! God the Father Almighty, I love you! God the Father Almighty, I love you! Amen." Alleluia!

Saint Francis of Assisi Speaks

My children, my brothers and sisters, my friends in the Good News, I love you; listen to me well. Today, and for the rest of your life, remain in the Peace of Christ. Do not let anything trouble you, do not let anyone disturb your inner Peace (no matter what that person says or does), do not let the events of life take you away from Peace. For this profound and lasting Peace is inside of you, deep within your heart, and it will never leave you. If you depart from this Peace today, for one reason or another, come quickly back to it, working hard to keep this Peace deep within you in a growing phase, and most of all, bless the Lord our God for having given it to you through the Blood of the Cross. "Jesus, Son of the Living God, I love you! Jesus, Son of the Living God, have pity on me, a sinner! Amen." Alleluia!

Saint Francis of Assisi Speaks

My children, my brothers and sisters, my friends in the Good News, I love you; listen to me well. Today, dear little heart seeking Love, live on Love. Give much Love to all those around you, be aware and grateful for the Love that God has shown you since your birth — and even today by this Message of Love — and love God for Himself and in everything. For we all live in Him, on earth as in Heaven, thanks to His Love. The Heart of God, dear soul, is an immense Heart at the heart of everything. My God, My Eternal Father, my Creator, how much I love you! Amen. Alleluia!

I say unto you, I say unto you verily, give me all your worries today, and in its place, insert God's Plan which will be revealed very quickly before your eyes. Amen. Alleluia!
~ Saint Francis

Saint Francis of Assisi Speaks

My children, my brothers and sisters, my friends in the Good News, I love you; listen to me well. Today, my dear soul in my hands, the hands of the humble father of the Friars Minor, rest and give me the burden of your life. Be light, be free, be simple, be without yesterday or tomorrow, be in the Holy instant that is life with Christ, our Lord and our God, and with us, your friends in Paradise. Rejoice over my Benediction, over the One of the Father, the Son, and the Holy Spirit, and delight in the prayer of gratitude that your heart will inspire you. I love you. I am Saint Francis of Assisi and I love you! Amen. Alleluia!

My children, my brothers and sisters, my friends in the Good News, I love you; listen to me well. Today, forget everything you think is your reality. Forget your past, present, and future, forget your position and your social status, forget your home and the city where you live. In the Eyes of God, these do not matter. Today, be a child of God, His beloved child, and today begins a new life for you. God knows exactly what route to have you take in order to bring you back to Him. Let Him guide you toward Himself, surrender yourself to your Creator, He Who is Supreme Wisdom, Exalted Love, Divine Welcome, Infinite Mercy. Give yourself fully, perfectly, and eternally to God, through our Savior, our Lord Jesus Christ, and the Immaculate Heart of Mary. I love you. Amen. Alleluia!

Saint Francis of Assisi Speaks

My children, my brothers and sisters in the Good News, I love you; listen to me well. Today, dear heart, I invite you to spend the day with me in Paradise. Yes! Imagine the high mountains, flower gardens, enchanting trails, and birds singing with us eternal praise to the Father! Imagine that I walk with you all day, that I hold your hand, that I keep you close to me, that I whisper the answers to all the questions that you ask yourself today, my dear soul, and believe in it because it is the truth! I will assist you all day, my little heart in my hands, and your day will be filled with promises fullfilled and Miracles received by the Grace of God, which is given to you today, my dear soul, through my Holy Soul and the Divine Providence that is protecting you. Amen. Alleluia!

14   Saint Francis of Assisi Speaks

My children, my brothers and sisters, my friends in the Good News, I love you; listen to me well. Today, my friends very dear, will be a very special day for you. Why? Because the Father Almighty will enter your life in an extraordinarily intimate and personal way at the level of your soul. Yes, dear little soul in search of God, God will manifest Himself today in your life in an unexpected, Powerful and Miraculous way, and leaving no doubt about the Truth of my Divine Words and the Holy Origin of the Teaching you are getting here through the books in this collection. For God the Father Almighty Himself designed the books in this collection and used His Messengers in Heaven as on earth to deliver them to you, and this, in a grand gesture of Love and Mercy for humanity. Today, dear heart, God Himself will confirm the Sanctity of this work, which is destined for you. Let us thank God for so much Mercy unto your life. Amen. Alleluia!

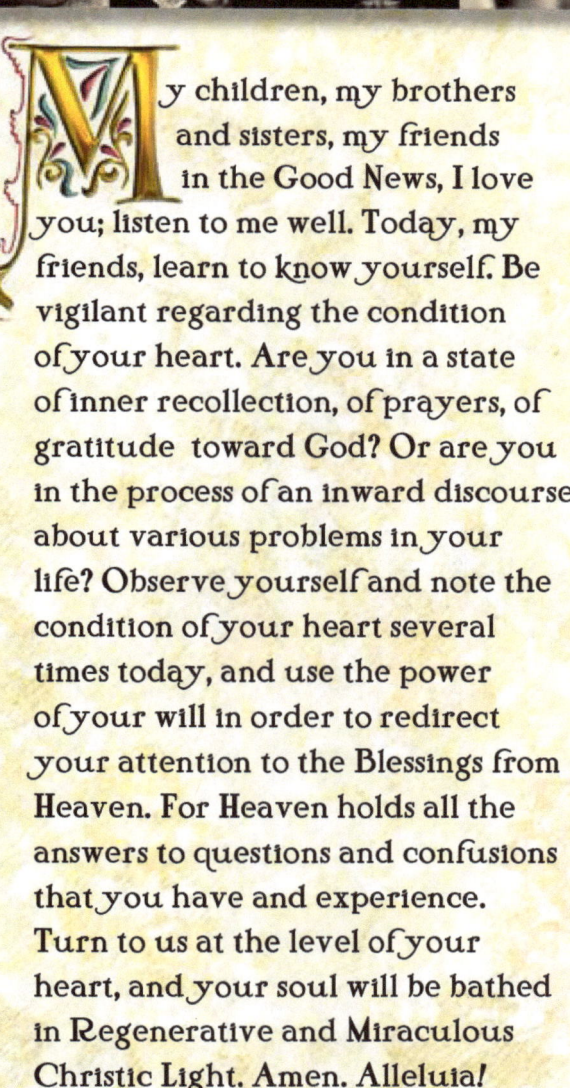

My children, my brothers and sisters, my friends in the Good News, I love you; listen to me well. Today, my friends, learn to know yourself. Be vigilant regarding the condition of your heart. Are you in a state of inner recollection, of prayers, of gratitude toward God? Or are you in the process of an inward discourse about various problems in your life? Observe yourself and note the condition of your heart several times today, and use the power of your will in order to redirect your attention to the Blessings from Heaven. For Heaven holds all the answers to questions and confusions that you have and experience. Turn to us at the level of your heart, and your soul will be bathed in Regenerative and Miraculous Christic Light. Amen. Alleluia!

Saint Francis of Assisi Speaks

My children, my brothers and sisters, my friends in the Good News, I love you; listen to me well. Today, dear heart, take away from your mind any preconceived notions of what tomorrow will bring. Live in the present moment, live in the Holy instant that is life with Christ, without worrying about the next minute, the next hour, the next day, the next year, etc. Surrender yourself completely and calmly to the Will of Christ, which is at One with the Will of the Father, and everything will fall into place for your soul's best. It may be that there are sudden changes in the road ahead, of minor or major adjustments in your life. If this is the case, be quite sure in the depth of your heart that this new scenario is of Divine Origin and that the new order in your life will serve you in a Miraculous way. For God's Plan is the only one that works flawlessly and brings you back to Him the fastest! Amen. Alleluia!

Saint Francis of Assisi Speaks

My friends, my brothers and sisters, my friends in the Good News, I love you; listen to me well. Today, my dear heart, stay calm. May the Peace of Our Lord be with you! The Lord protects you, the Lord loves you, the Lord is with you for the rest of your life — and beyond! Satan and his tenebrous aides can do nothing against you unless you say Yes directly to their invitations toward perversity, lies, abuse, neglect, materialism. Follow in the footsteps of Christ, stay comfortably in loving contemplation of the Cross, incline your head when you talk to God with humility, and the Heaven will open for you always and forever. Amen. Alleluia!

Saint Francis of Assisi Speaks

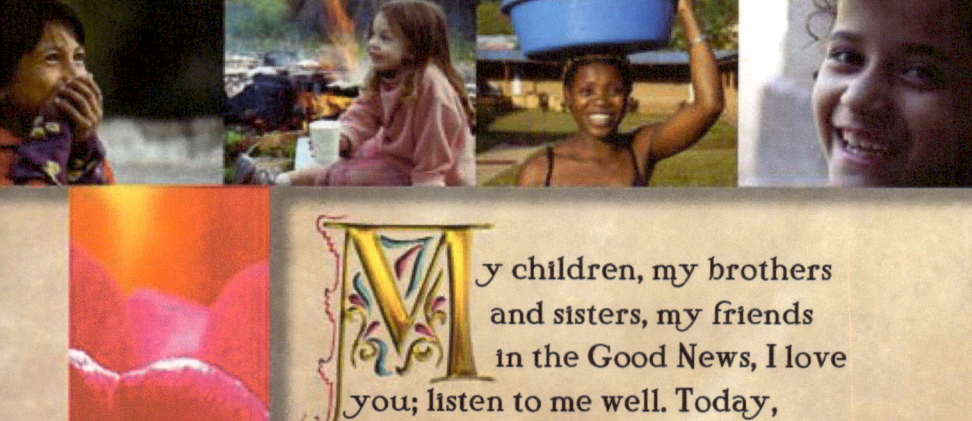

My children, my brothers and sisters, my friends in the Good News, I love you; listen to me well. Today, dear heart, rejoice and be glad! Be happy, for Paradise is given to you! Whatever tribulations of life on earth, unexpected and difficult events, mood changes of your friends or family members, regardless of life on earth thus, Paradise is given to you! So, dear heart, dear soul in my hands, get yourself a beautiful gift today from God the Father Almighty and be happy! Smile! Look at everything with joy and positivity! For life on earth is short and all your troubles will be rewarded after the passage that is death. Welcome to Paradise! Amen. Alleluia!

Saint Francis of Assisi Speaks

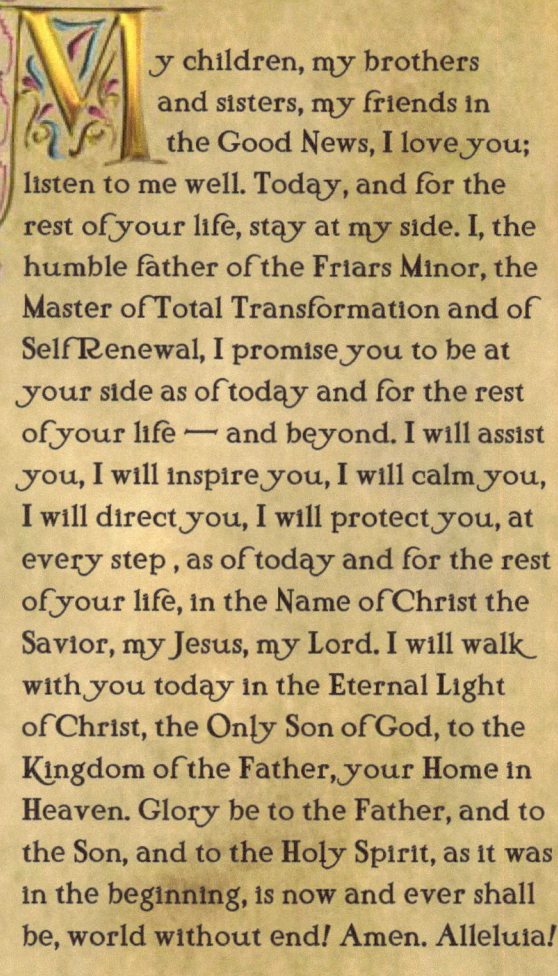

My children, my brothers and sisters, my friends in the Good News, I love you; listen to me well. Today, and for the rest of your life, stay at my side. I, the humble father of the Friars Minor, the Master of Total Transformation and of Self Renewal, I promise you to be at your side as of today and for the rest of your life — and beyond. I will assist you, I will inspire you, I will calm you, I will direct you, I will protect you, at every step, as of today and for the rest of your life, in the Name of Christ the Savior, my Jesus, my Lord. I will walk with you today in the Eternal Light of Christ, the Only Son of God, to the Kingdom of the Father, your Home in Heaven. Glory be to the Father, and to the Son, and to the Holy Spirit, as it was in the beginning, is now and ever shall be, world without end! Amen. Alleluia!

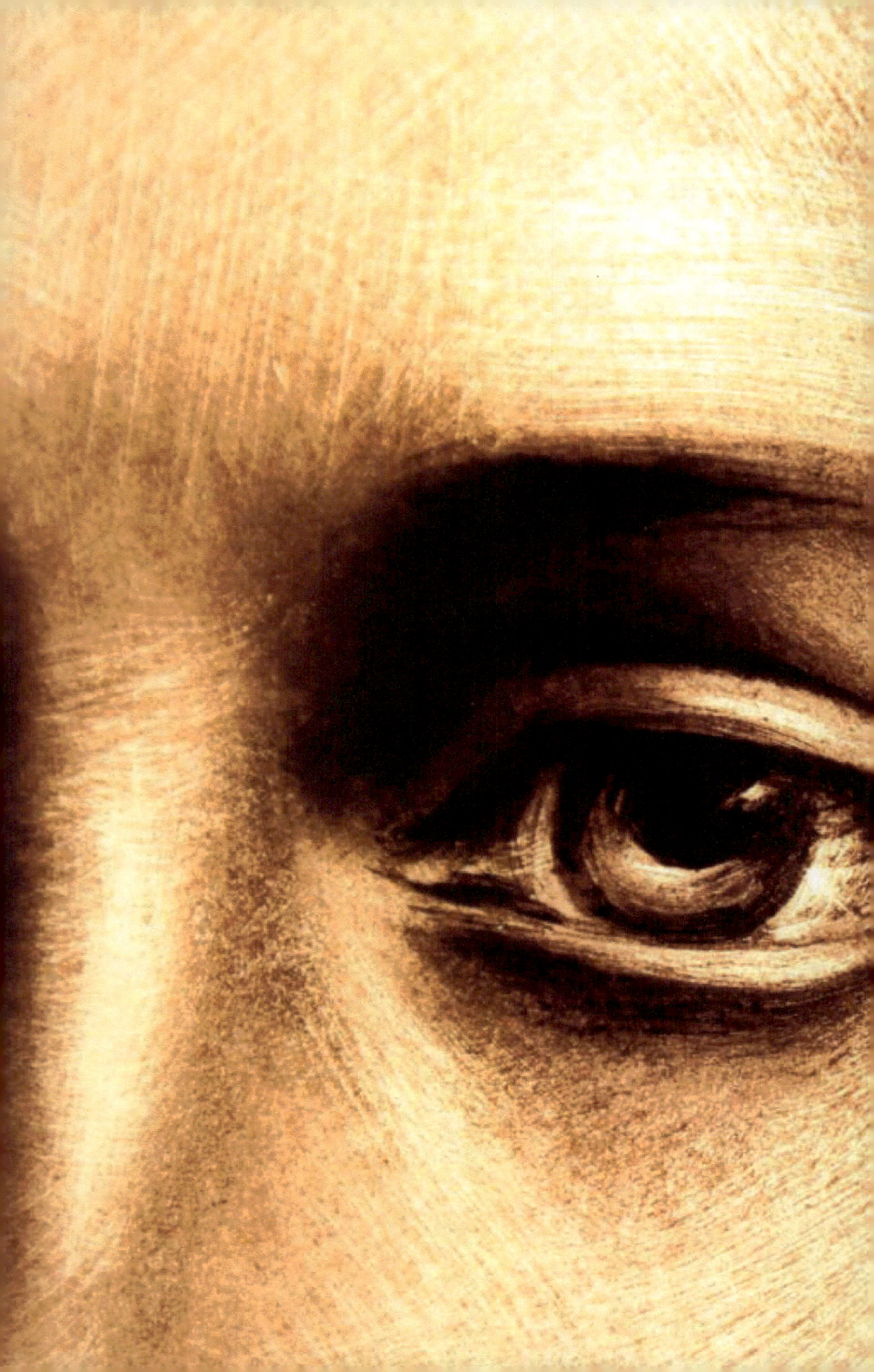

Saint Francis of Assisi Speaks

My children, my brothers and sisters, my friends in the Good News, I love you; listen to me well. Today, my dear heart, stay and remain in the Light of Christ. Your soul is sweet in the Eyes of the Father, especially when you bathe in the Light of His Son our Savior! Walk toward Him, our Jesus, our Christ, our Lord, and throw yourself into His marvellous Arms of Love and Tenderness for you! He is always there with you — in front of you — and He waits patiently for your awakening to Him. Holy! Holy! Holy! is the Lord God of Hosts! Blessed is he who comes in the Name of the Lord! Amen. Alleluia! I love you.

Saint Francis of Assisi Speaks

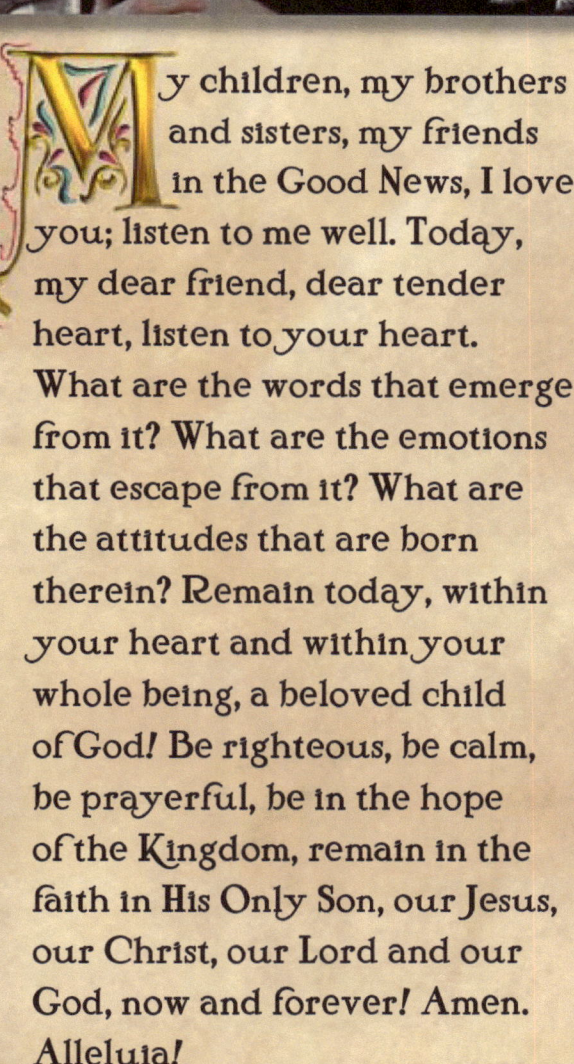

My children, my brothers and sisters, my friends in the Good News, I love you; listen to me well. Today, my dear friend, dear tender heart, listen to your heart. What are the words that emerge from it? What are the emotions that escape from it? What are the attitudes that are born therein? Remain today, within your heart and within your whole being, a beloved child of God! Be righteous, be calm, be prayerful, be in the hope of the Kingdom, remain in the faith in His Only Son, our Jesus, our Christ, our Lord and our God, now and forever! Amen. Alleluia!

My children, my brothers and sisters, my friends in the Good News, I love you; listen to me well. Today, my beloved of Love, be Love. Be in Love with your mission on earth; be in Love with Christ, our Savior and our God; be in Love with your little inner world (where I and other Saints of Paradise live with you); be in Love with this humanity in decline and toward whom you are charitable out of Christian Spirit; be in Love with the Eternal and Almighty Father, our Creator; be in Love with the Holy Spirit, your Guide and your Comforter; be in Love with your Heavenly Mother, the Most Blessed Virgin Mary, Who loves you and protects you; be in Love with your Guardian Angel, Who follows you step by step for the rest of your life. Be in Love with the Love Who lives and grows in everything, for God is Love and God is everywhere since we all live in Him, the Bearer of everything. Amen. Love. Alleluia!

Saint Francis of Assisi Speaks

My children, my friends in the Good News, I love you; listen to me well. Today, my beloveds, I want you to heal your body. Any residue of the past that has damaged your body, any intellectual or emotional error that led to bitterness inside of you, every inner imbalance at any level whatsoever — give them to me. Today, my little beloved, I will heal your physical and psychic bodies of many negative aggregates that were grafted into them over the course of years. Today, my dear heart, I will heal you! Often say: "Saint Francis of Assisi, heal me, purify me, transform me, renew me, bless me! Amen." Alleluia!

Saint Francis of Assisi Speaks

My children, my brothers and sisters, my friends in the Good News, I love you; listen to me well. Today, dear friends, dear hearts, become all brothers and sisters. Finished are the small misunderstandings that plague the days; finished are the manipulations of all kinds that serve only the malicious plans of Satan; finished are the silences or screams that hurt more than you can imagine. Today, my beloveds, be reunited all together, in Love and Forgiveness, in Patience and Gentleness toward each other, especially in the Peace and Joy of Christ our Savior. Today, dear friends, you are given the Mercy of God in all your relationships with those you carry in your hearts. Honor the Mercy of God, be grateful for the Mercy of God, share this Mercy of God. Amen. Alleluia!

Saint Francis of Assisi Speaks

My children, my brothers and sisters, my friends in the Good News, I love you; listen to me well. Today, do not be preoccupied with your future. Do not think about the next minute, the next hour, the next day, the next week, the next month, the next year, etc. Leave all your future with me! Between my hands, the hands of the humble father of the Friars Minor, which are combined with those of Jesus Christ our Savior, your future is assured. You will always have everything you need to continue your journey on earth, which unfolds flawlessly according to the Divine Plan of God. Thus, dear heart, be in the moment, listen to my Instructions and those of Christ, read the Teachings provided in this collection of books, execute what is requested therein with faith and discipline, and shortly, very shortly, everything will be clear in your life. I am Saint Francis of Assisi and I love you. Amen. Alleluia!

Thus, dear heart, be in the moment, listen to my Instructions and those of Christ, read the Teachings provided in this collection of books, execute what is requested therein with faith and discipline, and shortly, very shortly, everything will be clear in your life. I am Saint Francis of Assisi and I love you. Amen. Alleluia!

~ Saint Francis

Saint Francis of Assisi Speaks

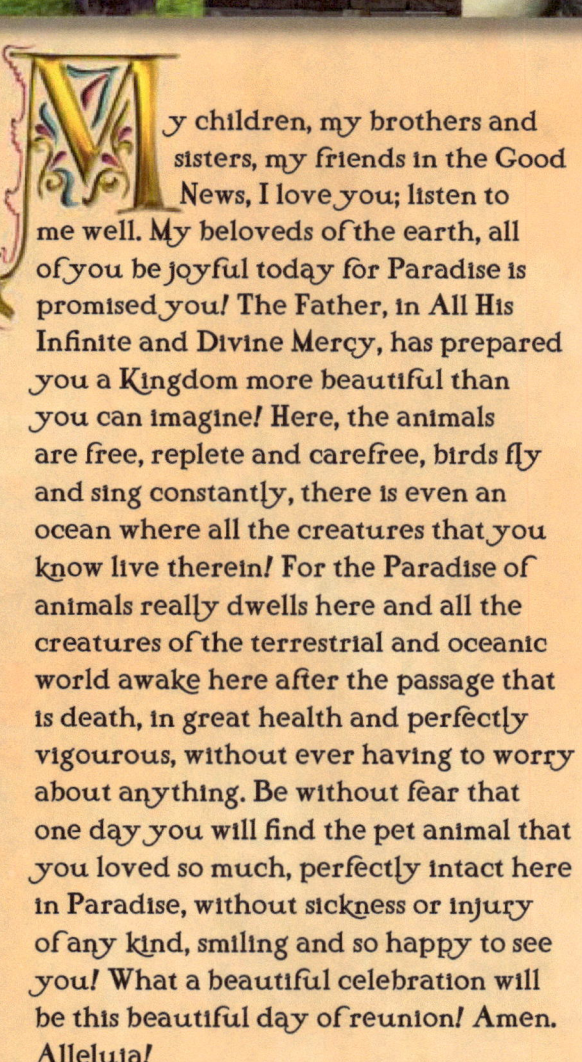

My children, my brothers and sisters, my friends in the Good News, I love you; listen to me well. My beloveds of the earth, all of you be joyful today for Paradise is promised you! The Father, in All His Infinite and Divine Mercy, has prepared you a Kingdom more beautiful than you can imagine! Here, the animals are free, replete and carefree, birds fly and sing constantly, there is even an ocean where all the creatures that you know live therein! For the Paradise of animals really dwells here and all the creatures of the terrestrial and oceanic world awake here after the passage that is death, in great health and perfectly vigourous, without ever having to worry about anything. Be without fear that one day you will find the pet animal that you loved so much, perfectly intact here in Paradise, without sickness or injury of any kind, smiling and so happy to see you! What a beautiful celebration will be this beautiful day of reunion! Amen. Alleluia!

Saint Francis of Assisi Speaks

My children, my brothers and sisters, I love you; listen to me well. Today, dear soul, be silent. What I mean by that is to listen solely to the voices and inspirations that come from your heart, and ignore the sounds, noises and shouts of the society around you. Stay in the citadel of your heart, in inner silence, in conversation with the inhabitants of Paradise only. Agreed? You will hear words and instructions clearly and precisely, much better than before. Direct your life of social interactions as you do every day; however, do not really engage yourself in them. Place your center of gravity, and especially what we call the awakening of your consciousness, in your heart. I will assist you. I love you.

Saint Francis of Assisi Speaks

My children, my brothers and sisters, my friends in the Good News, I love you; listen to me well. Today, dear heart in danger because you agree to it, rebel against yourself. Say No! to dark and negative ideas. Say No! to the so-called emotional traumas in your life. Say No! to the invitation of the ego to justify yourself in anxiety and depression for some reason or another. Why? Because your soul is now in my hands, those of Saint Francis of Assisi, joined with those of Christ, and my dear heart that I adore, nothing that is happening to you, today and for the rest of your life, can be harmful to you. Do you understand? I love you.

Saint Francis of Assisi Speaks

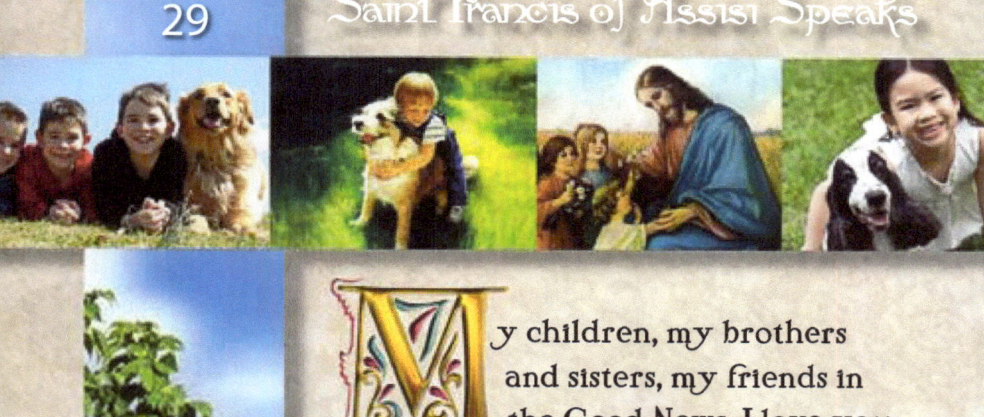

My children, my brothers and sisters, my friends in the Good News, I love you; listen to me well. The dramatic and accelerated changes in residence and work conditions, life plans that are made and unmade in a flash, and people coming and going in your life, are necessary results of your rapid spiritual and exponential growth. Trust us! Look back and see what you have accomplished so far! Heaven will not abandon you! Quite the contrary, Heaven is attracting you more and more rapidly, and the Peace and the Joy in Christ is given to you in an even more profound and lasting way every day. Rebel against yourself and say No! to any bad thought that contaminates your awakening consciousness. Smile! For Heaven is given to you today and forever! Amen. Alleluia!

Saint Francis of Assisi Speaks

My friends, my brothers and sisters, my friends in the Good News, I love you; listen to me well. Today, my beloved, be happy. The Joy and the Peace of Christ are given to you, dear heart; take them and make them live in your heart! It is so easy! Say Yes! to the spiritual life that is yours, say Yes! to the Cross that Christ asks you to carry (no matter what it holds), say Yes! to the Love of God which is clearly shown you. Say Yes! Yes! Yes! to the Kingdom of God awaiting you and whose Doors are now open for you! Amen. Alleluia!

My children, my brothers and sisters, my friends in the Good News, I love you; listen to me well. I wish today, dear child, that you would realize something very important. The life that is given to you, dear heart, is not yours. The house where you live, the car you drive, the clothes you wear, all of this is not yours. In addition, I would like to specify here that the life force that has animated you since your conception, dear child, is not of your doing, but it comes from God, by His Divine and Supreme Will. Do you see? Thus your life is not yours but belongs to God. Everything, absolutely everything you see around you, everything in the known universe of human beings,

everything in other worlds unknown to human beings, everything on earth as in Heaven (and beyond), belongs to God of which He is the Supreme Sovereign. For He decides everything about everything, at all times and in all places, in all known and unknown dimensions of men. Never doubt His ineffable Powers. Do not consider anything around you (or your own life) as your possession, and respect God in all His ineffable, inexhaustible, and immeasurably grand Plenitude. Give thanks today to God, Source of everything, Owner of everything, Governor of everything, Judge of everything, and most importantly, Return of everything. I love you. Amen. Alleluia!

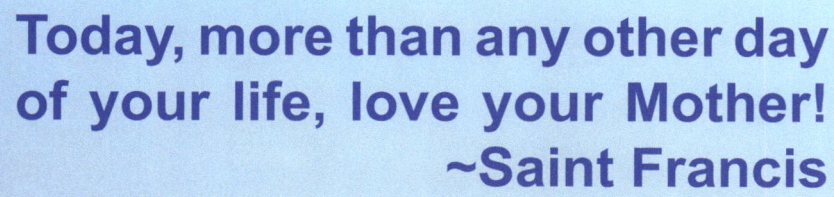

Today, more than any other day of your life, love your Mother!
~Saint Francis

Saint Francis of Assisi Speaks

My brothers and sisters, my friends in the Good News, I love you; listen to me well. Today, dear heart in distress, rejoice to know me. I, Saint Francis of Assisi, the humble father of the Friars Minor, the Master of Transformation and Renewal, am assisting you today and every day, in order to take you back as soon as possible and as quietly as possible to the Father's House, here in Paradise awaiting you. My Divine Faith, that is to say my Unique and Powerful Personality in the Eyes of the Father, allows me to grant you favors and Miracles that you could not get without my intercession. Do you see? So be thankful to God for my entrance and my permanent attendance in your life, dear heart, for it is God Himself Who has allowed it. I love you. Amen. Alleluia!

Saint Francis of Assisi Speaks

My children, my brothers and sisters, my friends in the Good News, I love you; listen to me well. Today, dear friend of my heart, rest in the Arms of Christ. Make yourself be One with His bleeding and triumphant Wounds; make yourself be One with His precious and marvelous Blood; dive head first into His Wounds and come out the other side refreshed, re-energized and strengthened. In Him alone you will find the rest you need; in Him alone you will find the profound and lasting Peace you are looking for. Today, my beloved, spend the day very very close to Christ, our Savior, our Lord and our God, Who loves you so much. Amen. Alleluia!

Saint Francis of Assisi Speaks

My child, my brothers and sisters, my friends in the Good News, I love you; listen to me well. Today, dear friends in the Grace of Jesus, our Savior God, be humble. Consider yourself the lowest of the earth. Realize in the depth of your heart, dear little soul in my hands, that the Father is much more intimate with you if you lower yourself to the rank of the least, as did His Son, Jesus our Lord. Humility is to know the state of one's soul in the Eyes of God. I love you. Amen. Alleluia!

Saint Francis of Assisi Speaks

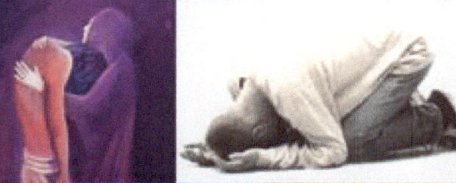  

My child, my brothers and sisters, my friends in the Good News, I love you; listen to me well. Today, be aware and repentant of all the wickedness that you have said or thought in your life, all the lies you have told or blathered to yourself or to others, all the decisions you have taken with your back turned to God and without regard for God. Be conscious and repentant; I repeat it: weep and bitterly regret silently in your heart for having offended God as often as you have, and ask forgiveness. Today say often: "I have sinned, Lord, have mercy on me. Amen." I love you and I will assist you. Amen. Alleluia!

Today say often: "I have sinned, Lord, have mercy on me. Amen." I love you and I will assist you. Amen. Alleluia!
~ Saint Francis

Saint Francis of Assisi Speaks

My children, my brothers and sisters, my friends in the Good News, I love you; listen to me well. Today, dear friends, dear hearts, be altogether brothers and sisters on earth. Help each other out! Bear with each other! Love each other! Forgive each other! Time passes so quickly on earth (I remember) and opportunities to reconcile with your fellow human being appear quickly and disappear just as quickly if you do not seize the opportunity given. You are obligated to help each other as taught by Christ through the Doctrine of Charity He has transmitted to His Apostles and which is written very clearly in the Gospels. To be worthy of what represents the life of a child of God as taught by the Gospel, you are obligated to love your fellow human being. For loving your fellow human being and loving God are one and the same thing. God the Father Almighty will judge you on this point. I love you.

Saint Francis of Assisi Speaks

My children, my friends in the Good News, I love you; listen to me well. Today, my dear friends, my dear hearts, protect yourself from evil spirits who prowl about the world seeking the ruin of souls. Wear a Cross around your neck, put a Cross over the door of your house (or all entrances), place beautiful relics of the Blessed Virgin Mary and of the Saints you love, as well as beautiful Crucifixes, all around your house. Display your beliefs, inspire yourself by viewing these Sacred objects, and especially increase the Christic Vibrational Energy of the environment where you live. This Energy of Protection will help you more than you think. For the battle for souls between the White Forces and the dark forces is already underway, dear heart, in other worlds that you do not know, and those adverse and undesirable effects will increase more and more on earth at all levels. I will assist you. I love you.

Saint Francis of Assisi Speaks

My children, my brothers and sisters, my friends in the Good News, I love you; listen to me well. Today, dear friends, be at Peace. The Almighty Father surrounds you with a blanket of extraordinary Divine Protection; Christ is warming you with His Fire of Grace and Wisdom; the Holy Spirit enlightens you and shows you the path to follow. Nothing, absolutely nothing that is outside of you can harm you unless you consent to Satan in one way or another, more or less consciously. This is why it is important to eliminate the ego as completely and as quickly as possible, so as not to leave any door open inside your heart for the evil that is outside. Be firm in your faith, be fearless, be in the Peace of Christ, our Savior, Who is always with you. I love you.

Saint Francis of Assisi Speaks

My children, my brothers and sisters, my friends in the Good News, I love you; listen to me well. Today, dear friends, remain in the Joy and Peace of the heart! The heart contemplating Christ on the Cross can not fail despite the evil that has infiltrated the earth. The heart contemplating Christ on the Cross can not lose the battle despite the number of evil spirits who try to assault him. The heart contemplating Christ on the Cross has no reason not to be in Joy, for Christ is the Only True Source of Profound Joy. Keep the eyes of the heart firmly fixed on the Glorious Cross of our Lord Jesus Christ, our Savior to all, and the road to the Kingdom will seem today much easier and peaceful. I love you.

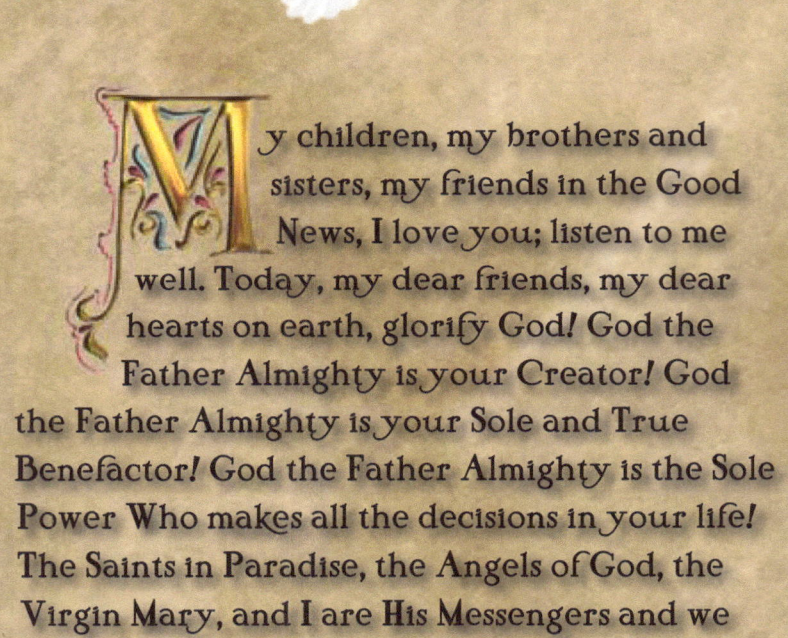

My children, my brothers and sisters, my friends in the Good News, I love you; listen to me well. Today, my dear friends, my dear hearts on earth, glorify God! God the Father Almighty is your Creator! God the Father Almighty is your Sole and True Benefactor! God the Father Almighty is the Sole Power Who makes all the decisions in your life! The Saints in Paradise, the Angels of God, the Virgin Mary, and I are His Messengers and we can not make any decision about you apart from

God. However, we can pray very hard for you! Oh, yes! And we pray for you more intensely and more frequently than you can imagine! Decisions that God makes regarding you, dear heart (and regarding all the creatures on earth), are influenced by our prayers in Paradise, your prayers on earth, and all the charitable works done on earth in His Name. Pray my friends, pray with us! And God the Father Almighty shall be Merciful unto you! Glory be to the Father, and to the Son, and to the Holy Spirit, as it was in the beginning, is now and ever shall be, world without end! Amen. Alleluia!

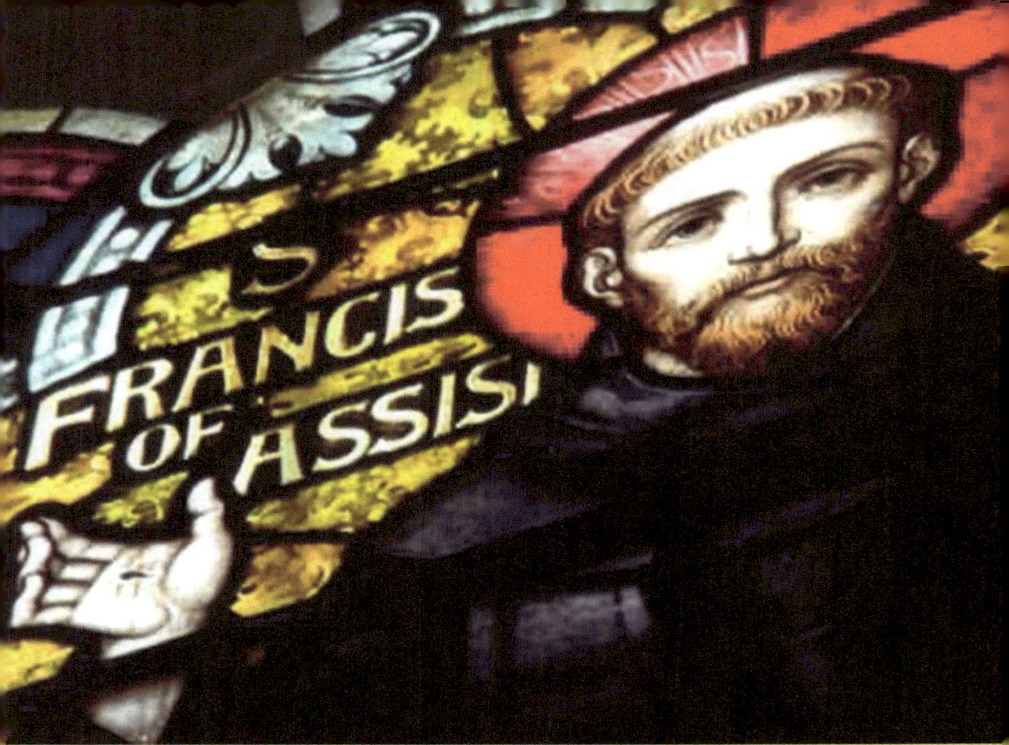
S
FRANCIS
OF ASSISI

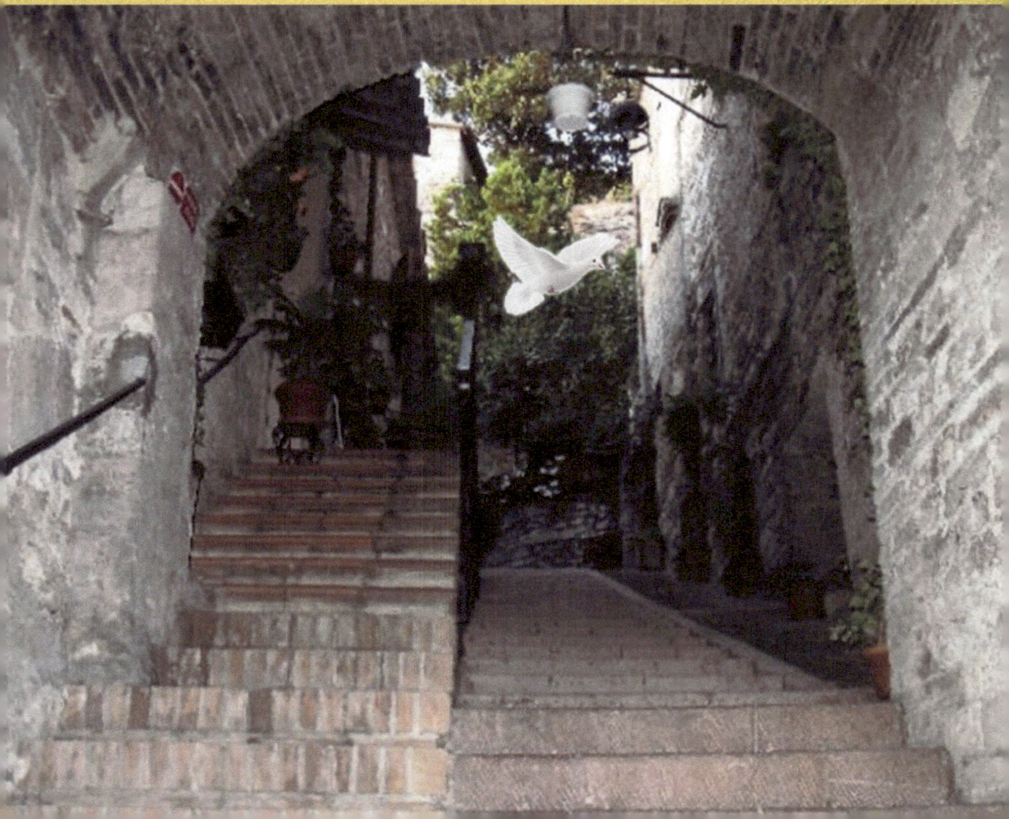

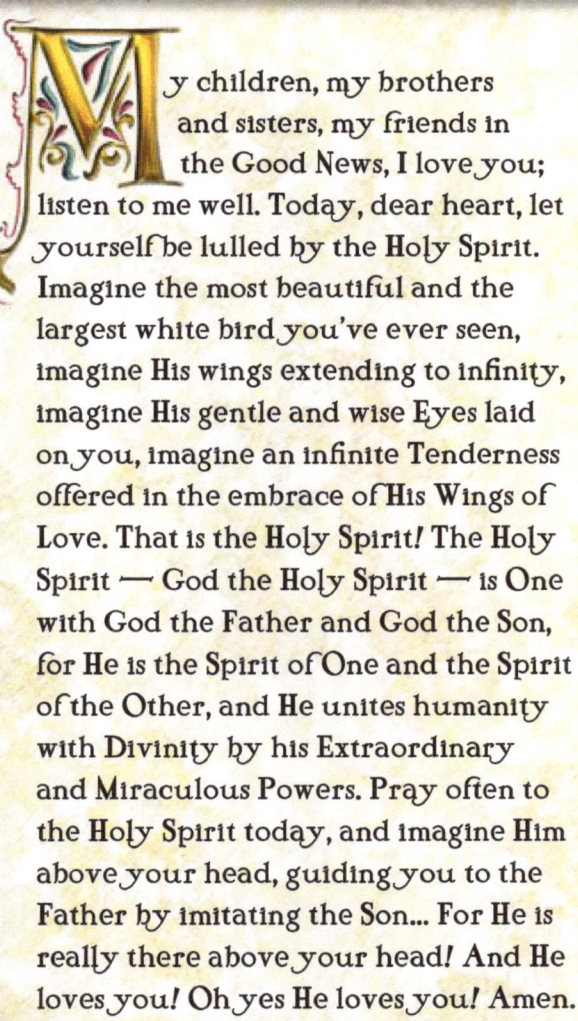

My children, my brothers and sisters, my friends in the Good News, I love you; listen to me well. Today, dear heart, let yourself be lulled by the Holy Spirit. Imagine the most beautiful and the largest white bird you've ever seen, imagine His wings extending to infinity, imagine His gentle and wise Eyes laid on you, imagine an infinite Tenderness offered in the embrace of His Wings of Love. That is the Holy Spirit! The Holy Spirit — God the Holy Spirit — is One with God the Father and God the Son, for He is the Spirit of One and the Spirit of the Other, and He unites humanity with Divinity by his Extraordinary and Miraculous Powers. Pray often to the Holy Spirit today, and imagine Him above your head, guiding you to the Father by imitating the Son... For He is really there above your head! And He loves you! Oh yes He loves you! Amen. Alleluia!

Saint Francis of Assisi Speaks

My children, my brothers and sisters, my friends in the Good News, I love you; listen to me well. Today, dear hearts in distress by the fluctuations of life on earth, listen well and put into practice the following precept: remain calm at all times...Remain calm in the midst of action as in the midst of resting, remain calm in your moments of interaction as in your moments of withdrawals, remain calm in your conversations with others as in your prayers, remain calm in the battles you are leading as in your moments of spiritual revitalization. Do you see? Remain calm at all times and in all places, and the inspiration brought forth by the Holy Spirit will flood you constantly with Wisdom and Charity, as well as the Strength and the Courage necessary for the success of your mission on earth. For your life is from now on a mission! Oh yes! I love you.

Saint Francis of Assisi Speaks

My children, my brothers and sisters, my friends in the Good News, I love you; listen to me well. Time passes quickly, my dear hearts. Life went on in a flash. There is no time to waste on frivolous and aimless thoughts or harmful emotions. Be master of your thoughts and choose the thoughts of Light and not those of darkness! Every second counts! I love you.

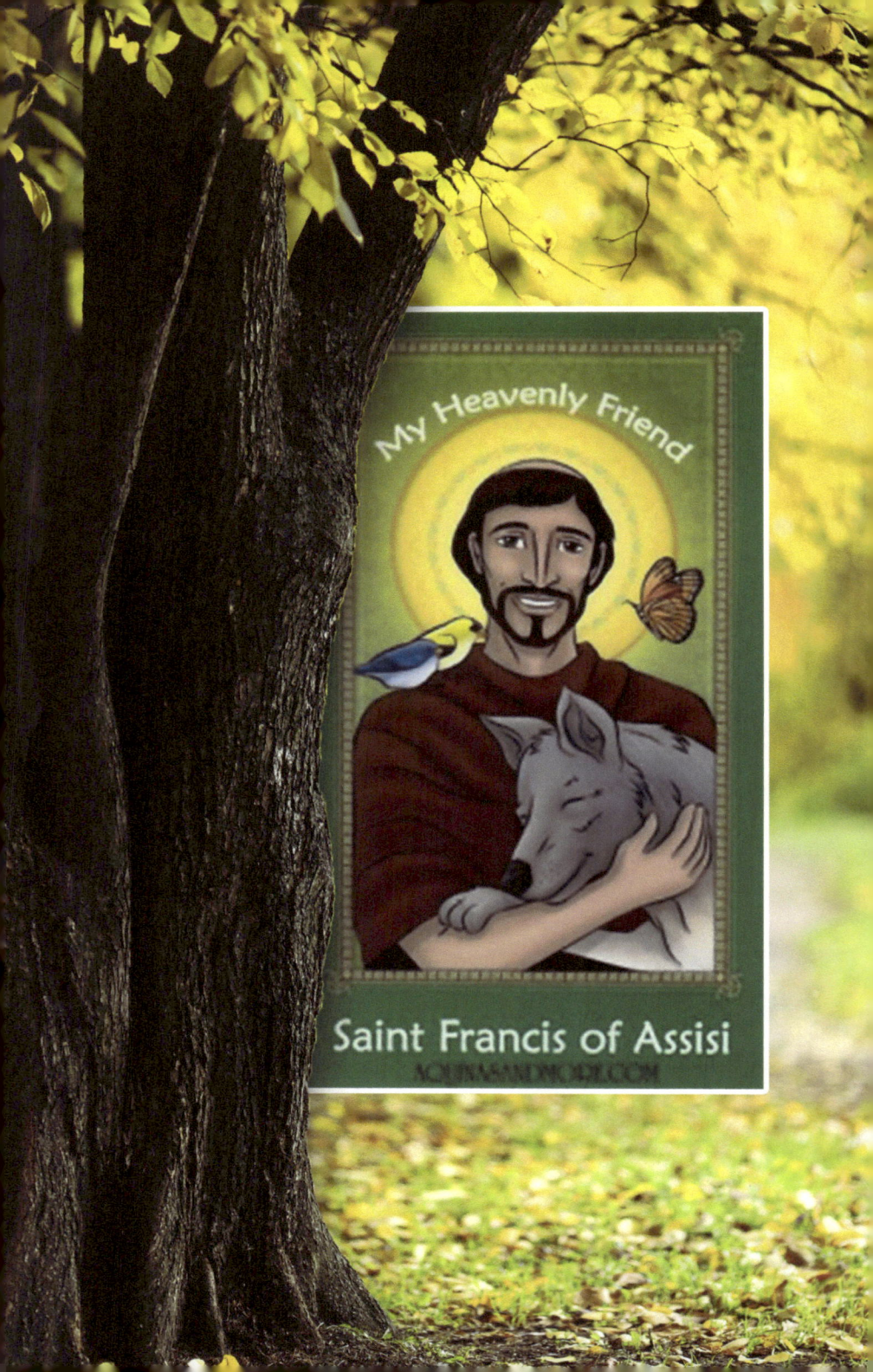

Saint Francis of Assisi Speaks

My children, my brothers and sisters, my friends in the Good News, I love you; listen to me well. Satan does not exist. By this, I mean that in Paradise from where I speak with you, Satan does not exist. In fact, he has already been forgiven and he has been exonerated of all his vices and all his cruelties. Outside of Paradise, however, and on earth in particular, Satan exists and he has more and more devastating effects on the souls, especially those weak and vulnerable souls without a firm foundation in God. To you, however, dear reader, Satan can do nothing because your soul is secure with us in Paradise. He will try to scare you, oh yes! But your soul is untouchable...And he knows that. That is why he struggles even harder to try to scare you! But do not worry, because from here where I speak (and where your Spirit lives), Satan does not exist. And your soul is perfectly secure in our hands, here in Paradise! I love you.

My children, my brothers and sisters, my friends in the Good News, I love you; listen to me well. Today, dear hearts, remember who you are! You are a child of God in exile on earth. The road will be tortuous, bad weather will be expected, and fatigue will overwhelm you. However, dear soul in my hands, assistance is given to you from Heaven! The Father has granted you assistance from the Saints in Paradise that you know through the books in this collection, as well as help from countless Angels in Paradise to assist you during your journey on earth. Each step you take is known to us, every decision you make has been inspired, and the resources you need to function are at your disposal. So, dear hearts, take heart and keep your eyes set on God Who is taking you back Home in His own way. Love your mission! I love you.

Today, dear hearts, remember who you are! You are a child of God in exile on earth.
~ Saint Francis

Saint Francis of Assisi Speaks

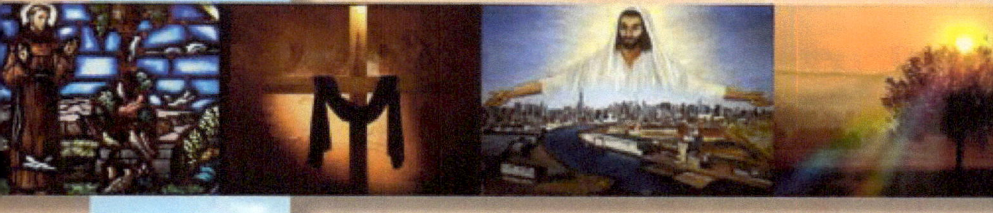

My children, my brothers and sisters, my friends in the Good News, I love you; listen to me well. I am concluding soon my Divine Teachings in these 2 books. I will speak with you again. Events that are fast approaching are not the end. Rather, they signal a brand new beginning. Be prepared, be grand, be strong, be in the Hope of the New Sun that will rise up very, very shortly. For God the Father Almighty has so decided.

I love you.

Saint Francis of Assisi
Humble father of the Friars Minor

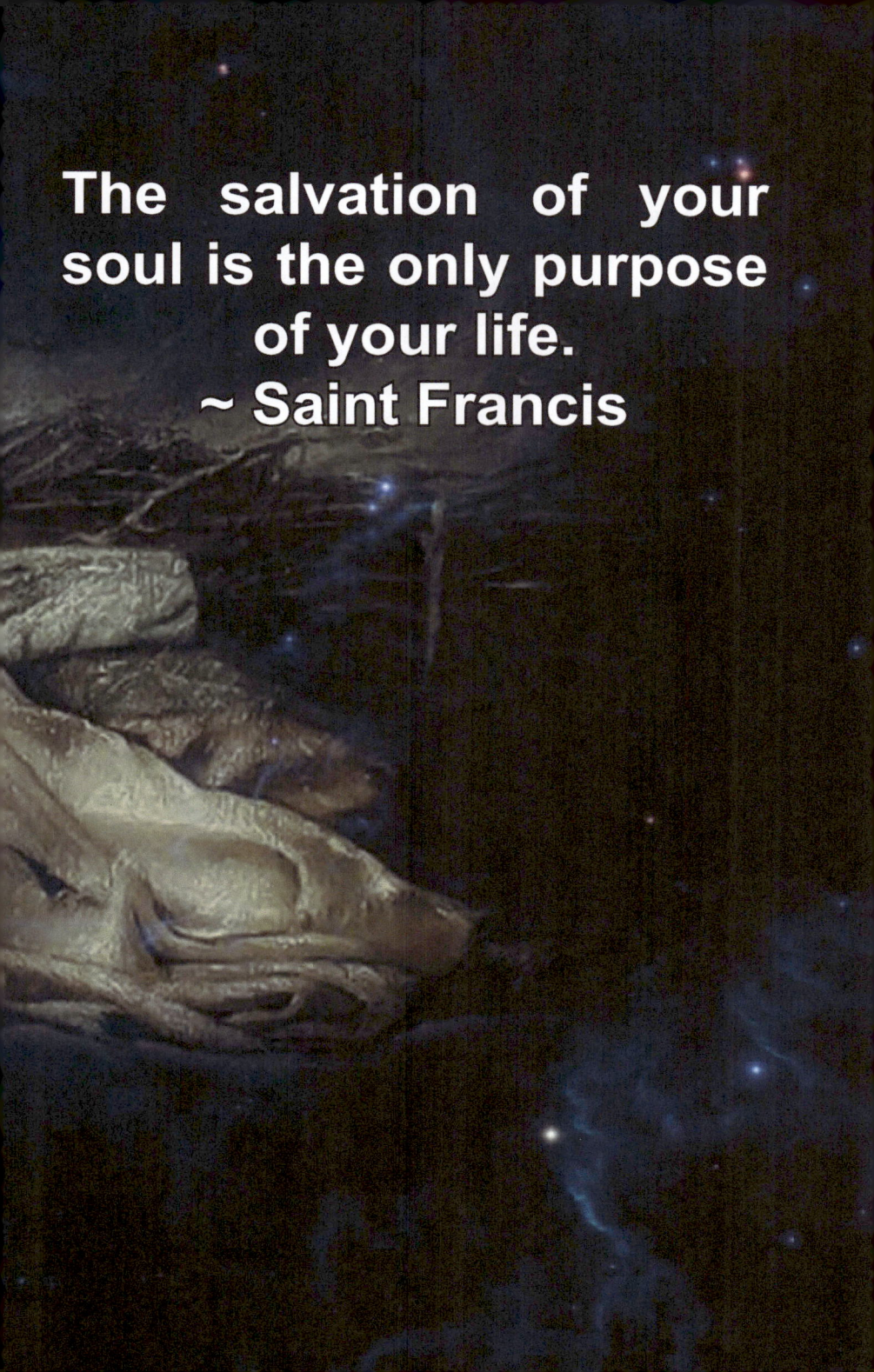

If you feel weak or unsteady, say this: "O God, come to my assistance, Lord, make haste to help me!"

~ Saint Francis

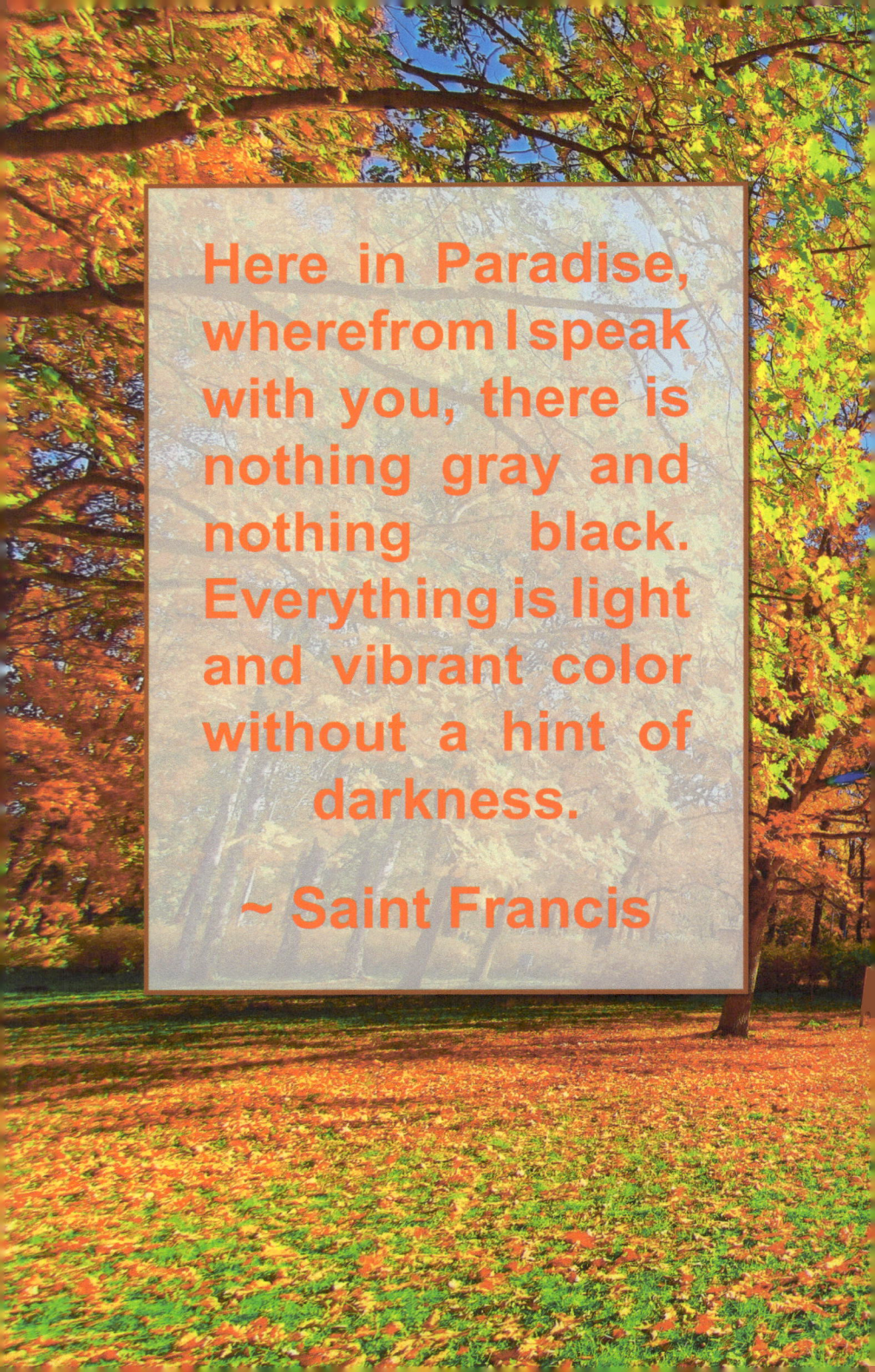

Here in Paradise, wherefrom I speak with you, there is nothing gray and nothing black. Everything is light and vibrant color without a hint of darkness.

~ Saint Francis

Afterword

I am always delighted to see my friend Francis visit me. He recently told me that he always accompanies Pope Francis and guides him personally.

May the great and humble father of the Friars Minor, Saint Francis of Assisi, also accompany you on your path returning back to the Father, as promised in this precious book.

Francis, I love you!

Marie-Josée

About the Author

Marie-Josée Thibault's life is in no way similar to yours. When she wakes, the saints of Heaven visit her, talk to her, teach her, and pray intensely with her. When such mystical sessions draw to a close, she greets with great respect and deep reverence the Masters of the Heavenly Court. This servant of the Lord spends the rest of the day in the company of her guardian angel, who continues her spiritual education and ceaselessly protects her from the perils of this fallen world.

Bestowed by the Heavenly Father, her gifts of clairvoyance and clairaudience allow her to remain in continuous contact with the supernatural dimension juxtaposed with ours, where the soul is born of the Spirit through Jesus and Mary. She prays that, one day soon, the entire human race will give glory to the Father, the Son, and the Holy Spirit.

Also by the Author

- Saint Padre Pio Speaks: Book 1
- Abba, Your Father, Speaks: Book I
- Abba, Your Father, Speaks: Book II
- Abba, Your Father, Speaks: Book III
- Angel Gabriel Speaks: Book 1
- Saint Beethoven Speaks: Book 1
- Dear Humanity: Book 1
- Dear Humanity: Book 2
- Saint Barnabas Speaks: Book 1
- Saint Bernadette Speaks Book 1
- Saint Therese of Lisieux Speaks: Book 1
- Saint Joan of Arc Speaks: Book 1
- Saint Martin de Porres Speaks: Book 1
- Saint John Paul II Speaks : Book 1
- Saint John Paul II Speaks : Book 2

MARIE-JOSEE THIBAULT

SAINT

FREE DOWNLOAD

Get your free copy of:
"Saint Padre Pio Speaks: Book 1"
when you sign up to the
author's VIP mailing list!
Get started here:

www.abbamyfatheriloveyou.com

BOOK I

www.ingramcontent.com/pod-product-compliance
Lightning Source LLC
Chambersburg PA
CBHW040455240426
43663CB00033B/20